For a Better Life

Christine Kohler

STECK-VAUGHN
Harcourt Supplemental Publishers

www.steck-vaughn.com

Photography: Cover ©Kurt Severin/Hulton Archive; p.iv ©Larry Chiger/SuperStock; p.2c–d Courtesy of Betty Gonzalez; p.5 ©AP/Wide World; p.6 ©Christine Kohler; pp.8–9 ©Bettmann/CORBIS; p.10a–b Courtesy of Adolf Neumann; p.13 Courtesy of Adolf Neumann; p.15 ©Reuters New Media/CORBIS; p.17 Courtesy of Vincent Hoang; p.19 Courtesy of Metty; p.21 ©David Guttenfelder/AP/Wide World; p.23 ©Christine Kohler; p.25b ©Bob Daemmrich/Stock Boston.

Additional photography by Corbis Royalty Free and Getty Royalty Free.

ISBN 0-7398-7508-6

Copyright © 2004 Steck-Vaughn, a division of Harcourt Supplemental Publishers, Inc. All rights reserved. No part of the material protected by this copyright may be reproduced or utilized in any form or by any means, electronic or mechanical, including photocopying, recording, or by any information storage and retrieval system, without permission in writing from the copyright owner. Requests for permission to make copies of any part of the work should be mailed to: Copyright Permissions, Steck-Vaughn, P.O. Box 26015, Austin, Texas 78755.

Power Up! Building Reading Strength is a trademark of Steck-Vaughn.

Printed in China.

2 3 4 5 6 7 8 9 M 07

Contents

Introduction
Refugees: Hear Their Voices..........................1

Chapter 1
Cuba: Operation Pedro Pan 2

Chapter 2
Europe: A War-torn Family.........................7

Chapter 3
Vietnam: A Country Split in Two..............14

Chapter 4
Africa: Power Shifts 19

Chapter 5
New Home, New Hope 24

Glossary 26
Index 28

Introduction

Refugees: Hear Their Voices

Refugees are people who seek to be free from fear. They leave their countries to be safe somewhere else.

Some refugees leave for fear of being hurt because of their race, who their friends are, their **religion,** or what countries their families came from long ago.

Some refugees leave because they are kept from practicing what they believe. They leave because they are scared of being locked up or killed if they do not agree with the **government.**

Read the refugees' stories. Hear their cries to be free. See how they took charge of their lives in a new land.

◀ The Statue of Liberty helps people remember what it means to be free.

Chapter 1

Cuba: Operation Pedro Pan

Men pointed their **guns** at the teachers. They ordered the **nuns** out of the Catholic school in Cuba. Betty Gonzalez, age 12, and her friends were frightened by the men. The men were **soldiers.**

One soldier said, "From now on, we will teach you."

These pictures show Betty Gonzalez at age eight (left) and at age twelve (right).

The soldiers were acting on Fidel Castro's orders. In 1959 they had taken over the Cuban government. Castro had become head of the new government. He believed in **communism.** Communism is a kind of government in which the state owns all land, houses, and places of work.

When the soldiers let the children go, Betty and her little brother, Julio, ran home.

Their father said, "No more school!" He feared that the Communists would train his children to believe wrong ideas. Betty's father and mother had heard that Castro said children belong to the government, not to their families.

Life in Communist Cuba

Children who went to school were ordered to tell the government if their fathers or mothers said anything bad about Castro.

Castro's soldiers sent some boys and girls to live and go to school in **camps.** Lessons centered on communism.

3

Betty and Julio did their lessons at home. One day in 1961, their father and mother told the children that they would be a part of Operation Pedro Pan.

Pedro Pan is Spanish for Peter Pan, a boy in a story. Peter Pan flies to a pretend place called Neverland. In Operation Pedro Pan, a **priest** helped many children leave Cuba to be safe in the United States. Fourteen thousand children left Cuba between 1960 and 1962.

Betty and Julio's mother told them that they would visit the United States for a few months, until Castro was no longer the head of Cuba.

Flying to Neverland

At the **airport** a Cuban soldier took Julio's bag away. Julio screamed. Betty told him to be quiet. She was afraid the soldiers would hurt her brother. She and Julio got on the plane.

When they reached the airport in Miami, Florida, a priest and some nuns welcomed them. The priest drove them south to Florida City.

For two months Betty and Julio lived in houses run by the priest and nuns. Then Betty was sent to a boarding school in New York State. Julio went to a boys' school nearby.

They waited and waited to go home. They listened for news that Castro was no longer the head of Cuba. The news never came.

Betty met a girl whose father worked in Mexico. Betty asked her friend for help. The girl's father was able to get Betty's father and mother out of Cuba and into Mexico.

Many children flew from Cuba to the United States between 1960 and 1962.

From Mexico Betty's father and mother went to Puerto Rico, which is part of the United States. Betty, age 17, and Julio, 15, moved to Puerto Rico to be with their mother and father. It had been five years since they had been together.

When Betty grew up, she moved to Texas. Now Betty works at Catholic Charities, where she helps refugees find jobs. She also helps Spanish-speaking refugees build new lives in the United States.

Betty now helps refugees when they come to the United States.

Europe: A War-torn Family

Adolf Neumann grew up in terrible times. His family was German. He was born in the Ukraine on August 14, 1941. The Ukraine and Russia were parts of the Soviet Union. Communists ran the Soviet government.

World War II had started. Germany had taken over Poland and wanted to control the Soviet Union, too. German soldiers marched into the Soviet Union in 1941. Many people in the Ukraine hoped the Germans would free them from the Communists. Other Ukrainian people didn't want the Germans to take over their country, though.

7

This map, from before World War II, shows the many places Adolf's family passed through during the war. ▶

Life under communism was hard. When some of Adolf's uncles spoke out against communism, the Communists killed them.

In the snowy winter of 1943, Adolf's two older brothers got very sick. Ukrainians wouldn't give the boys **medical** help because they were German. The Germans wouldn't help the boys because they lived in the Soviet Union. Both boys died.

Leaving the Ukraine

By 1944 the Germans were losing the war. German soldiers began to leave the Soviet Union. The Neumanns planned to leave, too. They were afraid Communists would kill them because they were German.

In January 1944, the Neumanns gave a German soldier money to **sneak** them across the Danube River. They left the Soviet Union.

Life was hard for many people during World War II.

8

The family went from one place to the next, trying to stay ahead of the fighting. They passed through Poland, Czechoslovakia, Hungary and Romania. During the trip, Adolf's sister also died. Adolf was the only child left in his family.

A Family Torn Apart

One day in 1944, the Neumanns were at a train stop. Airplanes began to drop **bombs** around them. Adolf, his mother, his aunt, and his **cousins** jumped on a train to get away from the bombs. Adolf's father and uncle hopped on another train.

When the train stopped, German soldiers put Adolf, his mother, his aunt, and his cousins in a camp in Austria. German soldiers were called

Adolf and his mother (top) lived in a refugee camp. His sister (bottom) lived there, too.

Nazis. Nazis locked up millions of people in camps in Europe.

The Neumann women and children lived in the Nazi camp for one year. They did not know where the Neumann men were.

In 1945, World War II ended and British soldiers freed the people in the camp where Adolf lived. About 12 million people in Europe no longer lived in their own countries. The Neumann women and children had nowhere to go. The British soldiers let them stay at a refugee camp.

Together for Good

Adolf's mother and aunt finally found the Neumann men in another camp in Austria. The first thing Adolf's mother did was show Adolf's father their new daughter. She had been born in the Nazi camp. The Neumann family moved to another refugee camp in Austria. There Adolf's mother and father had two more boys.

11

Adolf went to school for four years in Austria. His family still had no home. All over Europe fires from bombs had burned the buildings and the earth. Europe needed to be built again.

The Neumanns wanted to move. Adolf's father learned that there would be a five-year wait to get into the United States. Still, he put his family's name on the list.

A few weeks later, a government worker called them. He said a farmer in Montana would pay for a German family to come to the United States. He wanted a family who had worked in the Ukraine and had four children. The Neumanns were the only family who fit what he wanted!

In November 1951, the Neumanns boarded a ship sailing for New York City. From there they caught a train to Montana.

By the time the train had reached Chicago, the family had eaten all the food they had brought with them. Because Adolf knew a few English words, his father gave him all of their money. Adolf walked to the dining car. He entered the kitchen. He held up his coins and said, "Apples. I want 13 apples." Adolf asked for 13 apples because that was the highest number he had learned to count to in English.

The cook sold Adolf twenty apples for his coins. The Neumanns ate apples all the way to Montana. There Adolf's family worked for the farmer.

Adolf became a United States **citizen** in 1961 when he joined the United States Navy. Today Adolf Neumann works for the United States government in Washington, D.C.

Adolf joined the United States Navy.

13

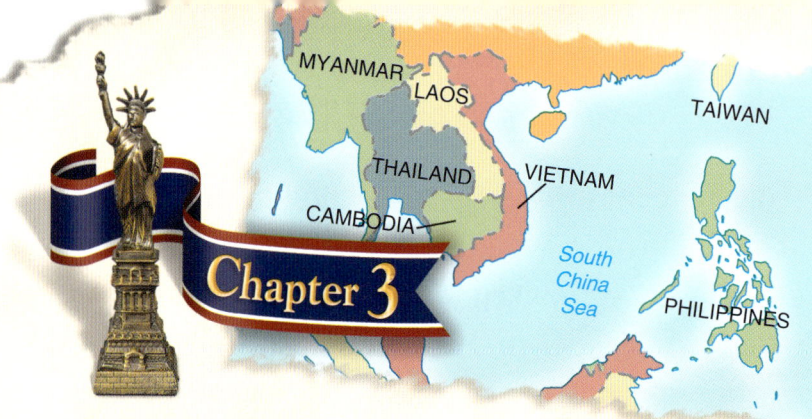

Vietnam: *A Country Split in Two*

The dark sky covered South Vietnam like a blanket. That night Vincent Hoàng, age 12, and his family would leave their country.

Ten years before, in 1975, Communists took over South Vietnam. They took over Grandfather Hoàng's store. They did not let the Hoàngs practice their religion. The Hoàngs were not safe. They had family who were soldiers fighting against the Communists.

Vincent's father had once been in medical school. He gave up his dream of becoming a doctor. His new dream was to get his whole family out of Vietnam. In 1981 he built his first fishing boat. He pretended to fish so he could sneak his family and other Vietnamese people to Thailand.

For five years Vincent's father sailed his 13 brothers and sisters out of the country a few at a time. Vincent's family, along with Grandfather and Grandmother Hoàng, were the last ones to leave Vietnam.

Vincent's father used a boat like this one to take his family out of Vietnam.

Taking a Chance

Vincent looked around his house one last time. They were leaving everything. He tapped his black-and-white ball with his foot. He loved to play **soccer.** He could get a new ball. Nothing could take the place of friends he was leaving behind, though. He would miss them.

The Hoangs sneaked out to their boat. Vincent's father packed 52 people into the 11-foot boat. They crossed their arms in front of them so they could all fit. They set out to sea, heading for Thailand.

Winds rose in the South China Sea. Waves grew as high as walls. By the second day, the storm was stronger. "No one would look for us at sea now," Vincent's father said.

On the third day at sea, high winds and big waves crashed against their boat. They thought it would be better to die in the ocean than at the hands of the Communists. Then an airplane flew over their heads.

"Whose plane is that?" Vincent asked.

"It's a Thai plane," his father said. He ran a white cloth up a wooden pole. Then he grabbed two babies and lifted them in the air to signal for help.

Vincent and his family were glad to be out of Vietnam.

Safe at Last

A Thai boat picked them up. The Hoàngs lived in a Thai refugee camp for six months.

Then they lived in a refugee camp in the Philippines for six more months. They learned to speak English. Vincent went to school. He played soccer again. He also learned a new game, table tennis.

Life was very different for the Hoàng family when they moved to the United States in January 1986. They had only lived in lands that had warm weather. When they got off the plane in Washington State, they saw snow for the first time.

At school many children made fun of Vincent because he didn't speak English well. The boys he met there didn't play soccer.

Vincent learned, like his father, that dreams sometimes have to change. Vincent practiced table tennis very hard. For two years in a row, he won first place in the table-tennis games at school.

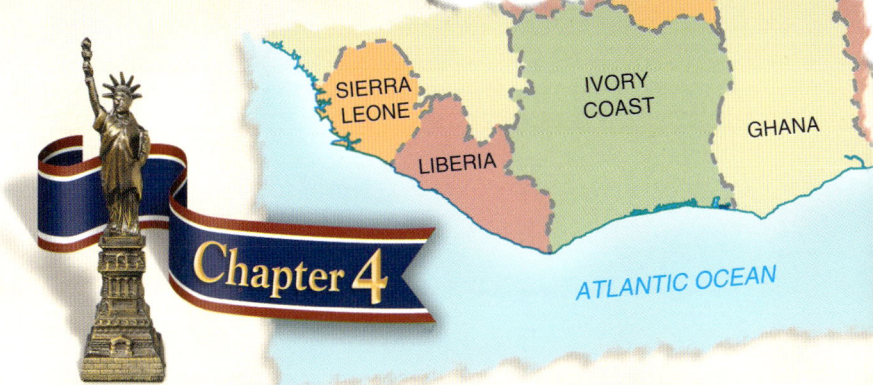

Chapter 4

Africa: Power Shifts

In Africa, 14-year-old Metty was like many girls and boys in the United States. She listened to music. She spoke English. She liked going to movies with friends. She played baseball and soccer. She helped her mother at home.

Metty, left, went to school at a refugee camp in Ghana.

Metty was living in a refugee camp in Ghana, Africa. Before living in the camp, Metty's home had been in Liberia, Africa.

In 1980 soldiers had taken over Liberia's government. Samuel Doe became the head of state. In 1985 he became President Doe. By December 1989 life was not safe in Liberia. Many people died fighting against the government of Liberia.

On September 9, 1990, Doe was killed by Liberian men fighting against his government. The next day Metty's family boarded a ship for Ghana. They feared for their lives because of all the fighting. About seven hundred thousand refugees left Liberia.

Life in a Refugee Camp

Metty's family lived in a tent during their first year in Ghana. Then they built a house from mud and sticks.

In the refugee camp, there were no jobs for Metty's father and mother. Other people were hungry, so Metty's family cooked and sold food at their house. Metty's sister raised chickens. Metty learned to cook outside. She cooked in a pan set on top of burning **coal.**

During the second year, Metty's father got sick. He left the camp to get medical help. His family never saw him again. Metty wanted to go back to Liberia, but there was no way to go back because of the fighting.

In the refugee camp, many people lived in tents.

A New Home Across the Sea

Metty's mother signed up to come to the United States. On March 21, 2001, her family flew to the United States.

"I hoped to see the wonderful United States," Metty, now 16, said. Her wish came true.

Metty's life changed after moving to the United States. In the refugee camp, she washed clothes in a stream. She rubbed them on a board. Today Metty uses a washing machine. Instead of cooking over coal outside, Metty now cooks on a stove in the family's kitchen. To take a bath in Africa, Metty used a pail to get water from a stream. She washed herself from the pail. Now she lives in an apartment with running water.

Metty's favorite game at school is tennis. Her courses are the same as they were in Ghana. Metty says that lessons are easier at her high school than at the Ghana camp. Still, Metty takes charge of her life by working hard to make good grades.

Metty said, "I write to my friends and say how glad I am for my life. I want them to come to the United States, too."

Metty likes playing tennis.

New Home, New Hope

Refugees from around the world have found a home in the United States. Many of them faced dangerous soldiers and oceans to get out of their home countries. Many refugees died trying to get to the United States. After many Vietnamese people died at sea, the United States made laws to help refugees.

There might be at least 13 million people in the world who are refugees, a United Nations paper stated in 1998. Today many refugees come to the United States from Africa, Asia, and Europe.

These people are becoming citizens of the United States. ▶

When a refugee fills out papers to live in the United States, government workers look into his or her past. The United States will not take someone who has done bad things.

After living in the United States for five years, the refugees can become citizens. When they become American citizens, they promise to be true to this country. Their new country has given them what they seek most. It has helped them become free and safe.

Glossary

airport (EHR pawrt) *noun* An airport is a place where airplanes land and take off.

bombs (BAHMZ) *noun* Bombs are things that are made to blow up and hurt people and things.

camps (KAMPS) *noun* Camps are places set up with houses or tents where people live for a short time.

citizen (SIHT uh zuhn) *noun* A citizen is a person who has full rights in a country.

coal (KOL) *noun* Coal is a black rock that burns when set on fire.

communism (KAHM yoo nihz uhm) *noun* Communism is a way of life in which the state owns all land, houses, and places of work.

cousins (KUHZ uhnz) *noun* Cousins are the children of one's aunt or uncle.

government (GUV uhrn muhnt) *noun* A government is a set of people who lead a country.

guns (GUHNZ) *noun* Guns are machines used to shoot animals or people.

medical (MEHD ih kuhl) *adjective* Medical means having to do with a doctor's care.

nuns (NUHNZ) *noun* Nuns are women who spend their lives working for something greater than themselves.

priest (PREEST) *noun* A priest is a person who spends his or her life working for something greater than himself or herself.

refugees (REHF yoo jeez) *noun* Refugees are people who leave their home countries because they are not safe there.

religion (rih LIHJ uhn) *noun* Religion is the practice of what one believes.

sneak (SNEEK) *verb* To sneak is to move quietly without being seen or heard.

soccer (SAHK uhr) *noun* Soccer is a game in which a team tries to win by kicking a ball into a net more times than the other team does.

soldiers (SOHL juhrz) *noun* Soldiers are people who fight for a country.

tennis (TEHN ihs) *noun* Tennis is a game played by two or four people who hit a small ball back and forth over a net.

Index

Africa 19–22, 24
Austria 9–12
Castro, Fidel 3–5
Cuba 2–5
Czechoslovakia 7, 9–10
Doe, Samuel 20
Germany 7, 9
Ghana 19–20, 22
Gonzalez, Betty 2–6
Gonzalez, Julio 3–6
Hoàng, Vincent 14–18
Liberia 19–21
Metty 19–23
Miami, Florida 2, 4
Montana 12–13

Neumann, Adolf 7–8, 10–13
New York City 12
New York State 5
Operation Pedro Pan 4–5
Peter Pan 4
Philippines 14, 18
Puerto Rico 6
Russia 7, 9
Soviet Union 7–9
Thailand 14–17
Ukraine 7–9
United Nations 24
United States Navy 13
Vietnam 14–15, 17